Printed in the United States of America.

Springer Literary House LLC
6260 Lavender Cloud Place
Las Vegas, Nevada 89122, USA

www.springerliteraryhouse.com

Lyrical Love

Poems of my Heart

VOLUME 1

Carlisa Riley

I decided to write poetry when I was dealing with a hard time in my life. It was a coping mechanism for me at the time. I would read my poems to my family and they would say "you should turn this into a book". The idea was silly to me at first. I'm not a poet, this is only for fun. The more poems I wrote, the more I realize my potential. Instead of saying how I felt, I allowed my pain to do the talking. Is there anything holding you back from healing? Do you still feel the pain from a certain time ago? Are you still fixing the heart that you didn't break? This is a special note to you that is saying, you're not alone. Your emotions are valid and you are heard. Diving into a world of loss and love, of hurting and healing, of caring and crying. These are the poems from my heart. Enjoy.

- carlisa riley -

I kept looking back trying to find you in the pass but in reality, you were no longer there

4/20/23

lyrical love (vol. 1)

We were just suicidal kids talking each other
out of committing. The sad irony of that

4/20/23

This world is too much for me yet it doesn't
give me enough
I want to see more but I've seen enough

I have a million thoughts which remain in my
mind
Everything is going so slow yet I never have
time

If you tell me I'm pretty I'll laugh in your face
as if you've offended me without any grace

If you tell me I'm smart I'll shed a slight smile
as if you said I have a mind that's vile

If you show me the love that I deserve I will
doubt your intentions and call you absurd

If you show me that you really do care I'll look
at you sad in hopes of despair

4/22/23

lyrical love (vol. 1)

Please don't tell me that you love me for that
I will ponder and stare at you blankly

Please don't show me any affection for that I
will doubt you due to neglection

Please don't tell me your favorite song for
that I will play it even when your long gone

Please don't allow me to share my heart for
that it will break when you tear it apart

4/22/23

My pass has taken over my present

If I go extinct will I still exist or will I
inevitably be thrown into the abyss

If I stay will I no longer be here or will I
wander this earth wishing I'd disappear

If I moved far away would my life become
better or will it fly away in the image of a
feather

And even when the clock strikes 11:11 I will
contemplate the wish of me being in heaven

4/22/23

lyrical love (vol. 1)

I would love to be loved
Heart filled with joy that even the bitterest of them
all could never destroy
What may I say to you when you say you love me?
What may I say to you when you say you hate me?
I love you they say to me,
you won't love me for long
I hate you they say to me,
well I knew it all along
You don't believe that I love you?
No I do not
Do you believe that I hate you?
Yes I do a lot
Can I prove to you that I love you?
I'll only shut you out in the fear of my doubts
Can I prove to you that I hate you?
I'll only let you in and which the cycle begins
What cycle they say, I don't understand they say
The cycle which starts with I love you and ends with
I hate you
The cycle that absorbs my hopes and desires for
which that love requires and inspires
The cycle that makes me question if love is real
The cycle that leaves me with no room to heal

4/22/23

We all love karma until it's reciprocated to us, then it's "life's not fair"

5/12/23

lyrical love (vol. 1)

At first I thought you were cute
I never thought me thinking you were cute was
going to leave my heart in pieces at the end

At first I thought you were funny
I never thought me thinking you were funny was
going to leave my heart in pieces in the end

At first I was in love with you
I never thought me being in love with you was
going to leave my heart in pieces in the end

You were my home
You were my safe place
The person I went to when I needed comfort
The person that I thought was going to be in my
life forever

You made me homeless
You made me be in fear
The person I steered away from when I needed
comfort
The person that's now a bittersweet memory

5/12/23

My love runs longer than any river
It dives deeper than any ocean
It's brighter than any sun
It's stronger than any weight
My lover is truer than any lie
My love rises more than the sun and the moon
My love grows taller than any sky
My love is more magical than any potion

5/13/23

lyrical love (vol. 1)

Love
That four letter word
That four letter word that can crush a soul or
make it whole
That four letter word that can fix a heart or tear it
apart
That four letter word that creates memories to last
for centuries or that can rain on parades to last a
decade

Love
That four letter word that brings people together
or pushes the ones away whom you thought
would be in your life forever
That four letter word that creates life but can
destroy it too
That can become old but also so new
That can make you laugh or make you cry
That can tell you the truth but can tell a lie
That can make you say the words "I love you" but
can also make you say the words "I hate you"
If love has ever taught me anything, it's that its
present one minute, then gone the next
If love has taught me anything, it's that you can
hear it in person, or see it over a text
If love has taught me anything, it's that it can be
quite and steady but also loud and heavy
That it can form future lives and create future ties
or destroy future fates and create future hate
Love
That four letter word

5/14/23

Love and Time

They both can be the same
They both hold value to their meaning and
name

Love and Time
They both can last
They both can come so slow but yet go by
so fast

Love and Time
They both can leave you behind
They both can become so hard to find

Love and Time
They both can stop
One can stop like a declining heart while the
other can stop like a broken clock

5/14/23

I'm clumsy

I am clumsy for love
I am clumsy to call someone my own
I am clumsy to do anything to not feel alone

I am clumsy for touch
I am clumsy to hear someone say you're not
too much

I am clumsy to hear the words I love you
I am clumsy to feel the emotions of love
I am clumsy for a lovers attention

I am clumsy to feel wanted
I am clumsy to feel appreciated
I am clumsy to feel loved
I am clumsy to be the first choice

I'm clumsy

5/16/23
Home

Home is not always a place

Home could be a scent
Home could be a memory
Home could be a person
Home could be a pet
Home could simply be… yourself

5/16/23

lyrical love (vol. 1)

What kind of love do you want?
The kind of love that devours your soul
The kind of love that never becomes old

The kind of love that sarantes your mind
The kind of love that elevates your time

The kind of love that awakens your care
The kind of love that fills your lungs up with
fresh air

The kind of love that massages your heart
The kind of love that can never fall apart

The kind of love that feels like the color
yellow
The kind of love that represents the word
Mellow
That's the kind of love I want

5/16/23

In my world, we survived
We overcame obstacles and we thrived

In my world, we were bright
We brought each other out of the dark even
when we couldn't see the light

In my world, you loved me back
You showed me the care my other pass
lovers lacked

In my world, you gave me attention
You gave me the attention I never had to
mention

In my world, I didn't have to lose you
I didn't have to have my heart broken in two

5/16/23

lyrical love (vol. 1)

I loved with a love that was deeper than the
ocean
I love with a love that was stronger than any
potion

I loved with a love that was longer than any
end
I loved with a love that was more innocent
than any sin

5/21/23

I'm scared this time

I'm scared that someone will actually love me
this time
I'm scared that someone will actually say
"you're mine"

I'm scared that someone will love me for me
I'm scared that I will be the only thing they see

I'm scared this time that I won't be a object
instead I'll be a beautiful project
I'm scared this time that I won't be a flaw
instead I'll be a work of awe
I'm scared that our love will come fast but go
by slow
I'm scared that I will leave since heartbreak is
all I know

5/21/23

lyrical love (vol. 1)

.

Your voice is like a sympathy to my ears
Your touch is a soft happiness to my skin
Your face is like art to my canvas
Your smile is a sunlight to my darkness

5/22/23

For you, I would have climbed the highest
summit for the endurance of your love
For you, I would have counted all the stars
that beautifully rested from above

For you, I would have shield you away from
any possible harm
For you, I would have been the person you
needed just so you could be in my your arms

For you, I would have listened to all of your
favorite songs
For you, I would have learned the lyrics just
so I could sing along

For you, I would have defended you from
anyone who spet upon your name
For you, I would have helped your flaws that
made you feel ashamed
For you my love, I would have acknowledge
d your biggest endeavor
And for you my love, I would have loved
you until the day after forever

5/22/23

lyrical love (vol. 1)

His face is a work of art, a work of art that
will be the canvas to my heart
His care is strength to my soul, it's stronger
than what any well of water could hold
His kiss is as meaningful as the word love,
love that sends me places with notes like a
beautiful dove
His hugs are like medicine to me, a cure that
will leave me feeling better and healthy

5/22/23

carlisa riley

If you were a candle, I would buy a dozen
of that same one and ignite them all. I would
ignite it in the winter, spring, summer, and
fall. You will catch me sitting by the candle
as it sheds its little flames, taking in the
sweet scent as the wax begins to grow a
dent. I would watch the flames as they sway
from left to right. I would watch the flames
decrease as the day falls to night. And as
the candle melts away in peace, I will light
another one to prevent you from becoming
ceased.

5/23/23

lyrical love (vol. 1)

Before I leave

Before I leave this world I want to live, not
survive but live
I want to not only receive happiness but to
also give
I need to feel the kindness of strangers auras
that pass me by on the street
I need to see the love between two elders that
would make you want to weep
I want to go back to old places that brings out
my childhood self
I want to feel amazing and wonderful feelings
that I have never felt
Before I leave

5/24/23

You were the creamer to my coffee
The sugar and butter to my toffee

You were the flame to my candle
The velcro straps to my sandal

You were the strings to my guitar
The away to my far

You were the features to my dove
The everlasting care to my love

5/24/23

lyrical love (vol. 1)

Fill me with love that only I can get full off of
Shower me in kisses that only I can get
cleaned from
Love me with love that only I can feel loved by

5/24/23

The moon and the sun
Constantly on the run
Catching a glimpse of each other as the
other one says goodbye
Being jealous of the stars that get to see the
other one from the sky
Being envy of those below that get to see the
other one glow
Feeling sorrow for themselves because thats
all they know
As the moon rises and the sun sets
They call out into the atmosphere, "not just
yet"
I need to see my sun shine bright
And I need to see my sweet moonlight

5/24/23

Romeo and Juliet
A Montague and a Capulet
Two star crossed lovers that longed for life
Two star crossed lovers whom ceased with a knife
Romeo oh Romeo, you are my Montague
Juliet oh Juliet, you are my Capulet

5/25/23

I want you to lick my wombs clean so they
can heal for you
I want you to patch my heart back up so it
can beat for you
I want you to clean my mind so it can be
clear for you
I want you to wax my soul so it can shine
for you

5/25/23

lyrical love (vol. 1)

They say if you love someone then you'll set them free and if they come back, then it was meant to be. And I never really believed in that saying. I thought it was stupid. I thought that if you loved someone that you wouldn't set them free because…you love them. But I think I finally understand that saying. That you love that person but you know you have to let them go, not because you love them but because you love yourself. But I don't really agree with the second statement. That you set them free and if they come back then it was meant to be. But if it was meant to be, don't you think you wouldn't have had to let them go in the first place? If it was meant to be they wouldn't have had to come back in the first place?

4/20/23

carlisa riley

As the sea calls out to the surface
What have I done to be away from you

As the surface calls out to the sea
You have done nothing to be away from me

As the sea calls out to the surface
I only get to touch you a little

As the surface calls out to the sea
At least we always meet in the middle
At least you get to take some of me back
with you
At least I get to absorb you as well
So my love, do not dwell

5/27/23

lyrical love (vol. 1)

If I were a flower, what flower would I be?
You would be a Daisy
If I were an animal , what animal would I be?
You would be koala bear
If I were a fruit, what fruit would I be?
You would be a banana
If I were a place, what place would I be?
You would be my home

Why would I be a Daisy?
Because you're simply as beautiful as one
Why would I be a koala bear?
Because your as cuddly and soft as one
Why would I be a banana?
Because your soul is as bright as the color
yellow
Why would I be your home?
Because you're simply, my home

5/28/23

It's not that you can't do it, it's just that you
allow fear to overtake you

5/28/23

lyrical love (vol. 1)

Money or Love?
She says love because love is already
expensive enough
He says money because times are already
rough

Money or Love?
She says money because think about how
much you could spend
He says love because love can last to the end

5/28/23

carlisa riley

You don't deserve to be gone
You deserve to belong

You don't deserve to perish
You deserve to cherish

You don't deserve to pass
You deserve to last

You don't deserve to be expired
You deserve to be desired

5/28/23

lyrical love (vol. 1)

Love me like a painter loves to paints
Love me like a singer loves to sing
Love me like a runner loves to run
Love me like a writer loves to write

5/28/23

carlisa riley

Your love has devoured me as of a kid
devourers a cake

Your love has pained me as of a head that
aches

Your love has comfort me as of a mother that
comforts her child

Your love has captured me as of a hunter that
romes in the wild

Your love has awakened me as of a person
does in the morning

Your love has enhanced me as of the meaning
for adorning

5/29/23

lyrical love (vol. 1)

I will love you until infinity stops
I will love you until the universe drops

I will love you until space turns bright
I will love you until definition of left means
right

I will love you until every star in the galaxy is
counted
I will love you until every painting in the
world is mounted

I will love you until my love runs out
And my dearest sweetheart, my love will
never run out

5/29/23

carlisa riley

I like the feeling of your head on my chest
Listening to the sound of my heartbeat as I rest

I like the sight of your captivating existence
Admiring it from a short beautiful distance

I like the comfort of your sweet kindness
That has no limit which that is so priceless

I like the kind of the magical love you show me
The kind that will forever go down in history

I like the presence of you being around
Close enough to hear the luxury of your
unique sound

I like the poetic answers of your intelligent mind
The ones that people search the whole earth
to find
I like the loudness of your outstanding loyalty
Bowing down before it like queens and kings
of royalty

5/29/23

lyrical love (vol. 1)

My heart was a prison
Your love was the crime

My care was change
Your love was a dime

My heart was a candle
Your love was the flame

My love was popular
Your love was lame

5/29/23

In the soft wintery night
I will never become cold due to your warm
presence

In the hot summer days
I will never become hot due to you cold
heart

5/30/23

lyrical love (vol. 1)

The things I would have done to just have
kept you in my life
The way I would have change things from
wrong just to make them right

The words I would have said just to be laid
in your bed
The problems I would have solved just so it
wouldn't stress your head

The facts I would have learned just for you
to be impressed by
The truths I would have sealed just so I
wouldn't hear you lie

The places I would have went just to fulfill
the day we spent
The love I would have gave just to have the
love that was meant

5/30/23

Your love is like a cup of hot chocolate
on a cold day
Your love is like the blossoming of flowers
in the middle of May

Your love is like medicine
for my sick body
Your love is like the calm music
that plays in a hotel lobby

Your love is like a soft cloud
that hangs in the sky
Your love is like a vibrant shirt
made of tye dye

Your love is like the shape
of the infinity symbol
Your love is like a flame
that I can constantly rekindle

5/31/23

lyrical love (vol. 1)

God has heard about you a thousand times
I just can't seem to get you off of my mind
I talk about you from day to night
I just can't seem to get you out of my sight

5/31/23

I used to feel pain and hatred when they said
your name
Now all I feel is calm and peace

5/31/23

lyrical love (vol. 1)

Call out my name as if you had no shame
Call out my name as if it were a game

Call out my name as if you were in pain
Call out my name as if you were insane

Call out my name as if I were to blame
Call out my name as if you weren't tamed

Call out my name as if you were framed
And for you my love I will do the same

5/31/23

carlisa riley

Tell me you love me and I'll shut every door
to my heart
due to being in fear of you possibly tearing it apart

Tell me I'm worthy and I'll run from you quickly
in hopes of dodging a bullet that will make
me sickly

Tell me you care for me and I'll go off and hide,
Preventing you from seeing the skeletons
that are inside

Tell me I'm valuable and I'll laugh until night falls,
thinking about what you said that made my
skin crawl

Tell me you want me and I'll push you far away,
in hopes that you leave for making you feel astray

Tell me I'm gorgeous and I'll say you're crazy,
wondering if you're serious or if you're just hazy

6/1/23

In another life, it'll just be me and you, I
promise

6/1/23

It's amazing how the most painful things
are silent

Like the breaking of a heart
The stream of a single tear
The loud thoughts of a mind

6/1/23

Karma
How it can be so charming
but shattering for some
Charming for those who wish revenge
on the next
Shattering for those who have done nothing
but tear and wreck

6/2/23

I crave the love that you see in books
The kind of love that reels you in like hooks

I crave the love that you see in movies
The kind of love that makes you feel groovy

6/2/23

lyrical love (vol. 1)

She is the light to my darkness
The giving to my selfishness
The paint stick to my art
The aorta to my heart
The wholeness to my soul
The achievement to my goal
The calming lyrics to my song
The right to my wrong
The solution to my strife
She is simply, the love to my life

6/2/23

He is the love to my hate
The guarantee to my fate
The clock to my time
The kind thoughts to my mind
The sapphire to my stone
The king to my throne
The eyes to my sight
The braveness to my fight
The words to my letter
He is simply, the longness to my forever

6/2/23

lyrical love (vol. 1)

You are not a box of darkness
You are a burst of sunshine

You are not a burden
You are sweet company

You are not disposable
You are valuable

You are not a dim light
You are a significant sight

6/3/23

We are all here for a purpose
Rather its good or bad
Happy or sad
Our purpose is significant
It all depends on what we do with it
Your purpose can change the world

6/3/23

Like the Perks of Being a Wallflower
once said…
We accept the love that we think
we deserve
Is it because we're not heard?
Is it because we feel absurd?
Or is it because we feel deferred?

6/3/23

carlisa riley

I'm not build for hookup culture
I love too hard
Give too much
And care too deeply

6/3/23

Billions of people in this world and I only
wanted you

6/3/23

As much as it hurt to see you walk away
It hurt more when you didn't look back

6/4/23

lyrical love (vol. 1)

Say you will you love me until the end
of times
To ease the mind that I call mine
hat I say is fine
But it's as sour as a lime sometimes a 10/10
like a dime but it can become blind or fall
behind or it can climb to it's prime which can
be a sign that it's becoming devine like light
of sunshine that becomes tasteful as wine
that calms you down to a feeling of divine to
feeling afloat like a swine to finally feeling
aligned and designed

6/4/23

Tell me I'm the one that you love
so I can feel above
Like a dove flying thereof the feeling
of dancing in a club to the rhythm flowing
like blood which is thick as mud or high
as a flood
That grows like a flower bud to that expands
like suds to make shiny as a singular stud

6/4/23

Your comfort person shouldn't be the one
making you uncomfortable

6/4/23

If the world were to ever end
I will be by your side through thick and thin
I would be your ride or die
For you I would tell the truth or lie

6/4/23

Things shouldn't make who you are, you should make who you are

6/6/23

My love for you is a longer
than the Mediterranean sea
My love for you is as higher
than Mount Everest
My love for you is wider
than the Tarbela Dam
My love for you is more powerful
than the human mind
My love for you is stronger than
Nuclear Pasta
My love for you is more
than yours ever will be

6/6/23

lyrical love (vol. 1)

Dance like your favorite song is playing
Laugh like you've just hear the funniest joke
in the world
Explore like you're on your dream vacation
And live like there is no tomorrow

6/6/23

Feeling in the void that has left me annoyed
therefore I avoid the things that I have
destroyed that I have once enjoyed

6/6/23

lyrical love (vol. 1)

Take the heart that I give to you in hopes
you won't turn it blue for which it will no
longer be new and it's time would be due for
repairing to bearing the feeling from caring
but also daring of me to risk my heart that I
painted like art for only you to tear apart to
stabbing it with a dart that will take me longer
to fixed and now my emotions are mixed that
I wish I could put to a nix but sadly I can't
instead my love will continue to grow like
a plant while your love will stay small as a
ant for that my friends will have to hear me
rant about the heart that I patched that can no
longer get attached to be snatched from me or
my prosperity

6/6/23

I want you to love me like I love you
But that means you'll have to love me first

6/7/23

lyrical love (vol. 1)

My beautiful soul that makes me whole
My gorgeous sight that creates my light
My captivating being that I don't mind seeing
My ethereal love that keeps me floating above
6/7/23

carlisa riley

You are the missing part to my life

The will to my might
The moon to my night
The sun to my light
The left to my right
The beauty to my sight
The calm to my fright
The landing to my flight
The inches to my height
The coffee to my delight
The armor to my fight
Again, you are the missing part to my life

6/7/23

.

lyrical love (vol. 1)

My heart is running in a race for you trying not
to slow down or stop, it sees the finish line and
the finish line is the love that I will receive back
from you but I need to reach it before someone
else will. The other hearts are running faster than
mine but I'm giving it everything I got, I promise
I'm running as fast as I can. I can see the finish
line. I'm so close. I don't look back, I don't want
to see the rest of the hearts behind me. I just want
to focus on that finish line. I don't stop for a break,
I keep running and running and running for your
love. I wonder if you're waiting for my heart at the
end or are you waiting for one of the other hearts.
I know you're looking to see which heart is the
fastest. That means, that heart tried the hardest
but I'm giving it everything I got, I promise I'm
running as fast I can. I can see the finish line. I'm
so close, I'm starting to pass the other hearts that's
ahead of me. I'm confident now, I'm going to win
this. That's when the heart behind me passes me by
again, No, no please I'm so close, I'm so close, it's
running too fast for me, so I begin to run faster, I'm
giving it everything I got, I promise I'm running
as fast I can. I can see the finish line. I'm so close,
I'm right behind the heart that's ahead of me. I can
see your love more than ever now. The other heart
ahead of me begins to run even faster. I'm giving it
everything I got, I promise I'm running as fast I can.
I can see the finish line closer than ever. The other
heart is too fast, no, no please, I was so close…I
was so close.

6/7/23

I crave for love in the most unwanted places
I look for care in the most unkind conditions
I long for touch in the most unloveable
situations

6/8/23

You are a sculpture of beauty that is captured
in an art museum

6/8/23

If I could talk to the word love, I would tell
it about you

6/8/23

lyrical love (vol. 1)

We love with our minds instead of our hearts
and wonder why our hearts get torn apart

6/8/23

Your love is a crime
And I'm willing to do the time

6/8/23

lyrical love (vol. 1)

She was the plant to my garden
He was the deal to my bargain
She was the sun to my shine
He was the belonging to mine

6/8/23

Are you the one I've been searching for my whole life
Or are you going to be the one to cause me strife

6/8/23

I was asleep until your love awaken me

6/8/23

carlisa riley

I was the sun and you were the beam
You were the sleep and I was the dream

I was the dove and you were the letter
You were the bird and I was the feather

I was the stars and you were the moon
You were the house and I was the room

I was the candle and you were the flame
You were the picture and I was the frame

6/10/23

We all our lost souls searching for our forever homes

6/10/23

You're very aware of things and that's why
you become hurt so much, therefore you
rather be oblivious to one's actions because
you think it will hurt less but in reality the
pain will remain the same

6/10/23

You ran away at the first sign of love in hopes
of falling in love

6/10/23

Things you love to do shouldn't become an obligation, it should become a choice

6/10/23

lyrical love (vol. 1)

Seeing you at first sight
Hugging you just as tight
Kissing you with all might
Having you with all right

6/10/23

carlisa riley

While it can rain on the most sunniest days
We can love in the most hateable ways

6/10/23

Sometimes were not enough for someone
That doesn't mean that we won't be enough
for someone else

6/11/23

No matter how hard it is to let go, you have to
The longer you hang on the harder it is to let go
Not saying that letting go should be easy, if it
were easy, then your love was never true

6/11/23

lyrical love (vol. 1)

It's amazing how a number of fortunate or unfortunate events connect us to the ones who will be in our lives forever. To think you met the love of your life because you were late for work

6/11/23

When it comes to love, I don't play.

6/11/23

lyrical love (vol. 1)

Love me like a beautiful song that makes you sing along that you play all day long without you feeling wrong for playing it so many times which you don't mind because you like the lyrics and how they rhyme

6/11/23

carlisa riley

My heart pumps for you
My mind thinks for you
My veins show for you
My nerves feel for you
My muscles bend for you
My bones grow for you

6/11/23

The absence of you love is overbearing
The heart you once loved is now tearing

6/11/23

carlisa riley

It's only at night when our hearts are heavy
And our minds are unsteady

6/11/23

lyrical love (vol. 1)

It was hard watching you walk away but I had
nothing left to say

6/11/23

This heart was once filled with life
That was until you stabbed it with a knife

6/11/23

All these years have passed and I still regret
that we didn't last

6/11/23

carlisa riley

Are minds are warzones
Are hearts are battles
Constantly in conflict with each other
You may have won the battle but you won't
win the war
I hearts might want it, but our minds always
seem to win

6/13/23

Love is unconditional…until it isn't

6/13/23

carlisa riley

You can pretend you don't care
But deep down inside you know you wished
it could have been different

6/13/23

lyrical love (vol. 1)

Our love is a chemical reaction
Changing and forming and
mixing and flowing over

6/13/23

carlisa riley

Every moment in our lives will be a
nostalgic memory, let's start appreciating the
present because soon we will start to miss it

6/13/23

You wanted me to let go and I wanted to
hang on
I wanted you here and you wanted me gone
You wanted me to say goodbye, while I
wanted to say hi
I wanted our love to be true
You wanted it to be a lie
I wanted to see us last
You wanted to leave us in the past

6/14/23

If you're scared that you'll catch feelings for someone, that means you've already caught feelings

6/15/23

lyrical love (vol. 1)

That's the thing about love is
It can be a beautiful work of art
Yet a tragic story that falls apart

6/15/23

carlisa riley

I treated you as my home while you treated
me as your dome

6/15/23

Happiness is the thing we all crave for, not
knowing that once we have it…we don't know
we have it

6/15/23

carlisa riley

Your love is like a cloud
Delightfully light but
heavily weighed
Gleefully bright but
reasonably dim

6/15/23

Sunlight creeps in as I caress your soft hair
taking within the fresh air with no despair, of
the night before knowing that I'm close to you
and only you

6/15/23

If you could just listen to your heart or mind
for one day, which one would you choose
and why would it be your mind?

6/15/23

If you could just listen to your heart or mind
for one day, which one would you choose and
why would it be your heart?

6/15/23

Sing me to sleep so
I count sheep so I can
dream about you and me

6/15/23

lyrical love (vol. 1)

I'm starving but not for food
I'm starving for
Your love
Your care
Your presence
You

6/15/23

I loved you too much
You loved me not enough
I wanted your touch
You cared of no such

6/15/23

I felt unknown for so long until you came
along and
made me feel like I belonged

6/15/23

Isn't it amazing how we desire things until
we have it?
How we long from love then spit on it when
we receive it
How we crave for money but use it out of
context when we get it
How we want valuable things but destroy
them when given to us

6/16/23

To think that one day you won't be here
doesn't sit right with me at all

6/16/23

Hi my love
Has anyone ever told you that you are ethereal?
That your surreal?
That you're unreal?
That your ideal?

6/16/23

lyrical love (vol. 1)

I'm in love with the stars
You are the stars and
I am the moon

6/16/23

carlisa riley

My love for you I will confess
With no rest and I will shout it
from my chest and I will give you nothing less
In hopes you won't think I'm a mess for trying
my best and in my arms I will build a nest as
you lay your head on my chest as I caress your
crest

6/16/23

Inside my mind is hollow
And on the outside I wallow
From self despair due to life being unfair
And I bathe in my depression trying to give out
reparation, to make me feel wanted but instead
I'm haunted by my woes that I have taunted

6/16/23

carlisa riley

Is it love or attention you crave?
Is it courage or strength that makes
you brave?
Is it hopelessness or worthless that makes
you give up
Is it happiness or conteness that fills up your
cup?

6/16/23

lyrical love (vol. 1)

He's beauty at first sight
Calming like the quiet night
His voice sings you to sleep
He wipes your tears as you weep
The touch of his skin makes you whole
The company of his presence fills your soul
His hugs will cure what nothing else can heal
He will make every standard you have
become real

6/17/23

The anger I feel is indescribable
The love I have is unreliable

The lies I tell are undeniable
The things I do is unrelatable

The goals I have are unattainable
The beauty I have is undesirable

The karma I get is indefinable
The company I need is unrealizable

6/18/23

lyrical love (vol. 1)

She is undeniably beautiful
Her smile lights up your day

She is undeniably gorgeous
Her touch warms your heart

She is undeniably captivating
Her care fills up your void

She is undeniably stunning
Her love heals your soul

6/18/23

The days seem hazy and my mind feels lazy

6/18/23

We might not be together, but at least we're
still under the same sun and moon

6/18/23

Winter and summer
Complete opposites
Coming and going
Cold on one end
Warm on the other
They never get to truly be together
Thank God for spring and fall
Helping them both feel a small amount from
another

6/18/23

All the pain and the world still spins

6/18/23

If you walk away my heart will
break and I can't that so please stay

6/18/23

lyrical love (vol. 1)

I broke myself just to fix you
I became old so you could become new

6/19/23

I have major attachment issues so if
I walk away,
Then you have really messed up

6/19/23

Our bodies are our homes
Let's keep them tidy

6/19/23

carlisa riley

Love is the gate to our hearts
Sometimes we leave the gate open
Sometimes we leave it closed
Sometimes we leave it crack

6/19/23

lyrical love (vol. 1)

My heart is blue from loving you
My heart is tearing from caring
My mind is dying from crying
My mind is lying from trying

6/19/23

Our love is a broken deal that I tried hard to
seal but our love wasn't real therefore I need
this time to heal from the heart you stole
that I let you hold but now its cold due to
your broken promise which makes you not
so honest and now I'm sad from all the bad
that's been shed on the care that you dare
say I didn't show which is below the truth
to the root but now I'm at ease and may you
please let me be so I can see the future thats
infront of me

6/19/23

lyrical love (vol. 1)

Feed me your lies so I can emphasize why
I can't trust and how you must realize the size
of your loyalty which is small and not tall and
you dig yourself into a hole which doesn't
make you bold but instead you fold and all I
can do is here you talk about the things I doubt

6/19/23

carlisa riley

During the night I'm a mess
I feel less like life's a test
And I can't rest because I'm constantly
studying
From the left to the right
With all my might but my brain feels tight
And so I turn off the light
But I can't sleep so I lay awake
Wondering how much more my mind can't take
Of overthinking and I'm mentally sinking
and I'm blinking the tears away hoping I get
to see the next day which for I would repeat
the constant defeat of my mind and my heart
constantly being torn apart

6/20/23

lyrical love (vol. 1)

Day by day I say it's okay
But I feel atray and like I'm they color
grey but I want to feel like May
and I want to badly stay and be a pretty display
But instead I decay and I carry more than I weigh
Therefore I lay thinking if I should pray for a
beautiful array that has yet come in my pathway

6/20/2023

In a perfect life it'll just be me and you
All brand new
Our time won't be due

6/20/23

lyrical love (vol. 1)

Loving you has cost me a part of my heart
That I will never get back and that's for a fact
And my heart that you attacked that make it lack
The potential and credential to be essential for
you but you turned my heart blue and for that I
can now say that I want you away

6/20/23

Life is too short not to tell the
person you love that you
love them, and life is too long to
be telling the person you don't love that
you love them

6/21/23

lyrical love (vol. 1)

It's moments like this that are special
The moments that make you laugh
That makes you dance
That makes you sing
That makes you feel simply happy

6/21/23

Moments when I feel alone
I wish I was gone
I wish I was unknown
I only cause wrong
I only feel prolonged
I feel like I don't belong
I feel like a sad song
My heart feels like a stone
My heart feels prone

6/21/23

lyrical love (vol. 1)

I know you're out there
Person that I haven't met
Person that I can't see yet
Our time is coming
I hope your running
To me of course
And I promise I'm running too
My beautiful unknown view

6/21/23

carlisa riley

We missed our time even
through all of the signs
I missed my time to call you mine
I say that I'm good when I know I'm not fine
I wanted you but I didn't fall in line
Maybe in the future we'll get to entwine

6/22/23

They say the worst thing you
can do is meet the right person at the wrong time
But what if you meet the wrong person,
but at the right time?

6/23/23

Lets rewire our love
It's been fading
and I've been waiting
For you to be all in
Before we come to an end

6/23/23

lyrical love (vol. 1)

I'll wait for you until the moon stops glowing
Until the trees stop growing
Until the Winter stops snowing
Until the mind stops knowing
I'll wait for you

6/23/23

carlisa riley

My heart wrote your name down
My mind captured your existence

My body remembered your touch
My voice song your name

My serotonin drew your jokes
My emotions painted your care

My pain sculpted your love
My peace molded your kindness

6/23/23

Don't let their failure fail you too

6/23/23

carlisa riley

He climbed mountains for me
while I moved them
He painted me paintings while I'll
hung them in art museums
He ran races for me while
I waited at the finish line
He grew plants for me while
I watered them
He kissed me as I
caressed his hair
He wiped my tears as I wiped his
He sketched me doodles as I shaded them in
He simply loved me as I simply loved him

6/24/23

I found peace inside of me
I'm proud of myself
I finally feel free
I look forward to the future
My power is stronger than ever
I can finally be me

6/24/23

Let's take a walk as we talk and lets draw
with chalk our love for another as we utter
kind words and lets hug each other tight
as we catch each other's sight and in that
moment when things feel right I'll whisper
how I love you and you'll say it back too
and my heart will feel new due to those four
but powerful letters that will never make a
heart blue but instead make a heart strong
and therefore live long

6/24/23

lyrical love (vol. 1)

Your beauty is lyrics to my eyes which is a
song I hide in disguise to prevent the outside
from seeing your beauty as well but I know
I shouldn't dwell and you should show off
your lyrics to the world so they can sing
along and be blown away and replay day
by day and they can say what a beautiful
song, which is your beauty that I shall stare
at and it's rare that you see such beauty that
causes no wrong so my love, show off your
beautiful song

6/24/23

My heart plays hide and seek from your love
The love you show me makes me scared
It's the good kind of love
It's just that I'm not used to it
You know, the good love, I'm not used to it
So be patient my love, don't give up trying
to find my heart
when it hides

6/25/23

lyrical love (vol. 1)

Your love is like summer, my love is a leaf,
and it grows for you on a tree in which in the
winter it falls for you, waiting until you come
back around. I shouldn't have to wait for your
love, but instead I do. As a leaf on the ground
I feel the coldness. My heart only gets you for
a season. I need your love for winter, spring,
summer and fall, so can your love be all those
for me?

6/25/23

I broke my heart fixing yours

6/25/23